GOVERNESS
POETRY & ILLUSTRATION

Kass Ghayouri

ISBN: 1500267872
ISBN 13: 9781500267872

Introduction

Poetry expresses essential elements. It enables the poet to express emotions using the art of writing. Poetry is complex and it emerges from the soul. It is the key to expose the imagination. Poet Kass Ghayouri uses speech and rhythm to articulate her thoughts. Poetry is her perception of reality. It is also the conception of her experiences. It is not just the experiences of daily life but also the experience of her vivid imagination and intellectual curiosity. Each verse projects her vibrant, vivacious, versatile vocal tone. Her imagination is like a visual slide creating images, with natural rhythm. With great brilliance, she bluntly and boldly expresses her intense feelings and opinions. She tactfully owns what she implies, sowing the seeds of intelligence in her poems. All forms of literary criteria dominate her poems. The poems embrace and embody all factors of life. It evokes all the five senses. In her mind she hears the melody of each poem. Her eyes capture images without resistance. The power of touch transcends from her heart. Like the taste of exotic spices, she tastes the bitter sweet moments of human consciousness. She is aware of what inspires and uplifts humanity. Kass Ghayouri is able to transport herself to a place in the universe, she sees as a spiritual dimension, capturing all aspects of the spiritual realm. She does not tamper with the spiritual world but through intense observation interprets the essence of its existence. Ideas leap into her mind and she is able to contemplate arguments through evidence.

Kass Ghayouri's academic poems need to be given special consideration. Her students and the academic environment extrinsically motivate her. She interprets education as a prime-learning tool, which enables students to flexibly apply knowledge in a given situation. The student is given the task to filter and interpret information provided by the teacher. Kass Ghayouri uses poetry as an alternative tool to educate and share knowledge. She demonstrates this unique technique in all her academic poems to make learning more effective. This confidently projects in her poems Essay Writing, Summary, Newspaper Article and The Literary Soup. She proposes other topics that she leaves open to interpretation and exploration.

Poetry enables Kass Ghayouri to blow off steam, yet not provoking a hostile response. However, it evokes the recipient to be empathetic and sympathetic to such distress. She airs her grievances and justifies her logical reasoning. Her evidence is clear and persuasive. Such conventions are evident in her psychological, social and motivational poems. Kass Ghayouri uses rules and conventions to adequately enhance her ability to express herself. She instinctively adopts a style and technique to pour out words in the form of poetry. Indeed, her poems display clarity and coherence. Instead of wading through pages to identify the argument she provides a lucid outline, in the form of a poem. Equipped with the fundamental knowledge, she takes the challenge to express such emotions in a flamboyant style. Therefore, this genre of literature enables Kass Ghayouri to employ her thoughts and ideas, aesthetically. It is fundamentally a creative way to express emotions, through her unique diction.

Table of Content

Academic
Issues

William Shakespeare
By: Kass Ghayouri

In the 1590's he wrote his plays,
In the 1609's sonnets filled his days,
Flamboyant plays in Elizabethan diction,
Poetry and prose enlightened with fiction,
Theatre provided the immediate needs,
Exposing Shakespeare's plays indeed.

Shakespeare wrote in poetry and prose,
Providing the audience with a comic dose,
His tragedies are characterized by doom,
His romance in a feigned state of bloom,
Iambic pentameter verse without rhyme,
Soliloquies are part of Shakespearean time.

Hamlet reveals a ghost from above,
King Lear projects filial love,
Macbeth reveals a tragic plight,
Romeo and Juliet families fight,
Twelfth Night exemplifies love that's great,
Othello demonstrates, revenge and hate.

Shakespeare brought English to life,
Widespread with vocabulary that is rife,
Stratford was his place of birth,
The early 1600's a great writer was placed on earth,
His plays were brought to the Elizabethan stage,
Flamboyant and extravagant costumes of that age.

His plays were performed at the globe,
The actor performed his soliloquy in a robe,
Followed by jokes, farce, and innuendo,
The antagonist, protagonist, hero and foe,
Historical plays, satirical comedies and tragedy,
Tragic comedy, Dramatic Irony and comedy.

Nelson Mandela
By Kass Ghayouri

Nelson Mandela is his name,
Fighting for justice is his game,
South Africa is his place of birth,
A hero is placed upon our earth,
The apartheid system he had to fight,
Because racism is just not right,
Lived in a cell like a little box,
The Afrikaner government as sly as a fox,
Mandela is the strength of a nation,
Trying to abolish all segregation,
Colour of skin determined his fate,
A land that spelled out so much hate,
Strong, stubborn, slender looking man,
On his movements there was a ban,
White Afrikaner Nationalist came to power,
Mandela fought for freedom hour by hour,
His release was so bitter sweet,
At 80 the apartheid system he beat,
Bang! Bang! Bang! Went the police gun,
Life in Roben Island was no fun,
Roben Island was a harsh place,
As tears ran down Mandela's face,
He could not even see his wife,
For his people he sacrificed his life,
He symbolized the word free,
His hands the branches of a tree,
His life was a roller coaster ride,
By apartheid laws he had to abide,
He emerged to change a country's history,
His life was such a serious mystery,
A country that felt the pain,
Freedom is what it aimed to gain,
Blacks were given the first vote,
South Africans could now gloat,
The Nobel Prize is what Mandela won,
To fix a nation that was torn,
Nelson Mandela brought upon peace,
After 27 years people saw his release,
The sight of South Africans in tears,
As the sound of the gun nears,
The smell of gunpowder in the air,
The taste of blood is just not fair,
Nelson Mandela touches my heart,
In our history he plays a special part,
A worst racial tyranny a world has seen,
For 27 years in prison Mandela had been.

Essay Writing
By: Kass Ghayouri

Formatting an essay plan,
Brainstorming ideas if you can,
Analyze and interpret the topic,
A moderate format to pick,
Outline a flowing structure,
According to the teacher's lecture.

Introduction designed to attract,
From the topic do not distract,
Define it in an explicit term,
A hook statement that is firm,
Illustrate the points you wish to make,
A good grade is at stake.

Thesis statement is what it's all about,
Do not keep your audience in doubt,
Compose and support the main idea,
Formulated thesis should be clear,
Last line of the introduction it sits,
Explicitly and implicitly it fits.

Opening statement in body one, two and three,
Let your explicit details run free,
Description, explanation and elaboration,
Introducing arguments in collaboration,
Closing statement in the next row,
Transitional statement adds to the flow.

Conclusion brings in closure,
Thesis statement is given exposure,
Stated in a different term,
Yet standing strong and firm,
Summary of all the points,
Transitional words connect the joints.

Plagiarizing is an offence,
Arguments need a strong defense,
Fulfilling all the specific stages,
Meeting the criteria of the pages,
Rules are a vital and integral part,
Make sure you follow it from the start.

An essay should be strictly formal,
Using contractions is not normal,
Eliminate the use of the word you,
Leave out questions in an essay you do,
Avoid the use of any slang,
No superficial details should hang.

Do not let it be a boring read,
It's a nerve wrecking activity indeed,
Always follow the writing rule,
Education is an important tool,
Proofread and edit all that you write,
Brainstorm ideas all through the night.

A Gifted Child
By: Kass Ghayouri

A sense of curiosity,
Interest with such intensity,
Powers of intense abstraction,
Excellent memory contraction,
Fluent and flexible thought,
Analytical reasoning sought.

Who is this gifted child?
Vivid imagination runs wild,
Excellent memory of a long term,
Into novels like a book worm,
Intrinsically motivated to learn,
Precocity is what they earn.

Projecting intellectual equanimity,
Qualities of prominent eccentricity,
Showing asynchronous development,
Leaving parents in bewilderment,
Not in sync with those of their age,
All part of their development stage.

First attempt at the gifted test,
A perfectionist projecting their best,
Unique and distinctive trait,
A gene that determined their fate,
Ability to learn so fast,
Crystallized memory that will last.

Escaping from the egalitarian society,
Distinct speech shows propriety,
Ostentatious linguistic speech,
Gifted child a pleasure to teach,
Always at the top of his class,
A ninety seven percent pass.

Newspaper Article
By: Kass Ghayouri

The heading has to be bold,
Byline is a journalist young or old,
Catchy subheading is next,
Newspaper an informative text,
First paragraph is called the lead,
A newspaper is important to read,
When, what, where, why, who?
How, should be addressed too,
When the incident took place?
Who are the people, culture, or race?
What was the problem at the scene?
Where have the victims been?
Why does the reader care?
At the fine print we stare,
Information paragraph in prose,
Reporting how the incident arose,
Reporting exactly what is seen,
A place where the journalist had been,
The paragraph is really short,
That's what a journalist is taught,
Factual paragraph reports what's true,
A witness may give us a clue,
Interview a person at the scene,
Stipulating what they really mean,
A witness, a police, mom or dad,
Feelings are gruesome and so sad,
Quotation marks state who speaks,
Personal and private information leaks,
It tells us that the news is true,
Witnesses are generally very few,
Summarize the article at the end,
Proofread, edit and then send.

A Summary
By: Kass Ghayouri

First read the entire text,
The step to follow next,
Understand the main idea,
Each paragraph should be clear,
Summarize it into one line,
Short paragraphs you can combine,
If the paragraph is long,
Three sentences are not wrong,
Now you have your notes,
Leave out examples and anecdotes,
Notes in a paragraph you do arrange,
Notes in a paragraph writing is not strange,
In a paragraph always indent,
Opening statement short in length,
Supporting details is what you need,
Finally, a closing statement indeed,
Transition words add to the flow,
Proofread and edit really slow,
Make sure your summary is not choppy,
Do not let your construction be floppy,
A summary should be rather short,
Trivial information you need to abort.
You have now drawn to an end,
A summary to your teacher you send.

Stairs to Success
By: Kass Ghayouri

Governess Academy is the school,
Gaining education is the tool,
Intrinsic motivation is what we need,
This will help us really succeed,
Ms. Kass gives us all hope,
With the curriculum we can cope,
Climbing those stairs to the top,
Gaining education will never stop,
Extrinsic motivation she will provide,
By her strict rules we will abide,
Etiquette manners we will receive,
Learning not to try to deceive,
Social skills are definitely a must,
Honesty, appreciation, kindness and trust,
From D to C to B and then to an A,
Academic education each and every day,
A school like this is one of a kind,
A teacher like this is hard to find,
She teaches from the bottom of the heart,
Giving students an excellent start,
Grade 1 to grade 12 knowledge we gain,
On our report cards good grades we will obtain,
Learning from our common mistake,
What good students we will make,
A loose cannon we will never be,
Education will always set us free,
Successfully these stairs we ascend,
And our grades will not descend,
She teaches us how to team play,
How to progress in the accepted way,
This is a school we will choose,
Because we have nothing to lose,
Governess Academy brings nothing but joy,
To each and every girl and boy.

Flashback Teachers!
By: Kass Ghayouri

Flashback to 1969,
Teaching was so fine,
Complimented on the task,
Putting on a teacher's mask,
Students were to blame,
When grades were so lame.

2014 has a new game,
Now Teacher's are to blame,
When a child gets a low grade,
Parents go on a vicious raid,
Like dogs they begin to bark,
Yelling about their child's mark.

She just cannot teach,
Parents begin to preach,
The teacher feels the stress,
The students create a mess,
"Mom, dad she does not like me,"
"Low marks as you can see!"

Flash back to that cane,
The student felt the pain,
Parents took the teacher's part,
"Make my child really smart!"
As the cane drew near,
The student felt the fear.

"I will work harder sir,"
Like a cat he begins to purr,
My apple I'd like to share,
Because you really care,
Thank you for making me smart,
In my life you have a special part.

Teachers leave my child alone,
I got him the cell phone,
To really monitor all about you,
And all that you do,
Now give him a break,
And stop acting so fake!

Don't yell or scream,
I will ruin your teacher's dream,
My child is really the best,
Give her an A on the test,
My child cannot fail,
The parent begins to wail.

Fast-forward to a cyber school,
A teaching robot is the tool,
The computer teacher teaches the child,
Studying is so fun and wild,
The parent has nothing to say,
Teaching so different from the olden day.

The Fugitive's Baby
By: Kass Ghayouri

An immigrant's unique tale,
Mother and baby under a veil,
Bravery and fortitude,
Travelling along latitude,
Across the Canadian Border,
Defying law and order.

A father's aggravated stress,
An ardent desire to caress,
Pursuit of welcoming his baby,
Will he survive maybe?
In a melancholic state,
Monitoring his heart rate.

Drove deeper into the storm,
Blizzard took a vicious form,
Wind continued to pierce,
The snow storm was fierce,
Variety of precipitation,
Father, mother, baby in a station.

Conquered their own fears,
As the Canadian border nears,
Beyond an infinitive universe,
Where life is uniquely diverse,
In the death of silence,
Risked imprisonment and violence.

Illegally embarked on a journey,
Defying the words of the attorney,
The ghostly silhouette of the jeep,
The baby could not cry or weep,
Psychological grief and physical pain,
A Nuclear family had lots to gain.

A Literary Soup
By: Kass Ghayouri

Personification is the ardent cook,
Alliteration adds repetition, rhyme, rhythm,
The **image** of them stirred in a pot,
Metaphor calls it a brutish tornado,
Stirring creates a wild whirling wind,
Aroma evokes the sense of smell,
Simile exclaims it's like a murky river,
Hyperbole calls it the million-dollar soup,
With the mixture of aromatic diction,
Analogy infers it's an unfortunate predicament,
Of the plight of vegetables assassinated in a pot,
The **antagonists** being **personification**,
Showing apathy to those vegetables,
Sadistically chopping them harshly,
Creating an empathic **atmosphere**,
The **protagonist** is the student,
Tasting the appetizing soup,
Alliteration scrumptious, savory soup,
Ironically the students eat the evidence,
Of the vegetables assaulted in a pot,
Foreshadowing it cannot be criminally wrong,
Substituting **literary devices** for vegetables,
The situation is such a **paradox**,
Chopping **figurative devices** in a pot,
Evoking **pathos** for poor vegetables in a pot.
This is an **anecdote** of a teacher,
Introducing students to the **literary** soup.

Time (The Essence of Time)
By: Kass Ghayouri

Time is our fundamental mood,
Approaching in a particular sequence,
Motioning the sun across the sky,
Stipulating the phases of the moon,
Recalling events of the past,
Appealing to views of the planet,
Fearing the future what time may bring.

Time eludes our physical beauty,
Adding dimensions to our body,
Placing itself in our lifespan,
Growing old in the age of time,
Shrinking, sagging, suppressing,
An operation definition of age,
The duration of life nears the end.

Simultaneously time is money,
Tick tock tick tock beats the clock,
The awareness of economic value,
As it drifts through the lunar months,
What an astrological experience,
Time synchronizes and tabulates our day,
Like a cheetah time leaps by.

Time adopts the valid name history,
Creating, destroying, and rebuilding,
Living through the duration of the time,
We postulate its period, process, point,
It's the phenomena of our existence,
We solve problems by evoking time,
We compromise the essence of time.

Then time becomes the antagonists,
As it is triggered by a timer,
Displaying its explosive force,
Dispensing fragments of shrapnel,
Time becomes vicious, vindictive, venomous,
Exploding like a volcanic eruption,
Jeopardizing the future of our planet.

The hypothetical time machine,
Motioning backwards and forwards,
Into a new physical dimension,
It finds its place in literature,
Our imaginations engage in time travel,
Violating the boundaries of time,
Creating a plot device in a fictional novel.

The English idiom face time,
Maintaining personal interaction,
Electronically, email, e commerce,
Time walks through our lives,
Illuminating all social alienation,
The psychological context of time,
The changing face of time.

Types of Teachers
By: Kass Ghayouri

A bumbler is the one that stumbles,
Like a toddler taking their first step,
Secretly, scratching, scrambling through the mess,
Of books and papers scattered on the table,
Gum flies out of her mouth while lecturing,
Like a missile it lands on the student,
Who explodes in a fit of laughter,
Laughter roars through the class.

Bumblers cannot focus on the task at hand,
Goes off the topic like a car skidding of the road,
Factual information is often wrong,
Exemplifying that she is not prepared,
Droopy, drowsy, dreamy personality,
Perpetually moves like a slow snail,
Cannot meet the expectations of the curriculum,
No constructive, collaborative culminating task.

The martinet is a teacher, who is strict,
A disciplinarian that has rigid rules,
Like a sergeant in the army they command,
Their voices, the sound of roaring thunder,
They rumble like an earthquake,
Their tempers are a magnitude of ten,
Trembling, terrified, tortured students,
The martinet creates an authoritarian climate.

The martinet gives a stern, staunch stubborn look,
Students withdraw into their shells like turtles,
Their insults sting like a swarm of bees,
A classroom of cold frozen statues,
The martinet calls out a student's name,
The student immediately jumps out of his skin,
The marks issued are notoriously low,
The test and exams designed to trick.

The professional teacher enters with poise,
Elite, elegant, ethical, etiquette, entertaining,
They project a deep passion for teaching,
The professional is so enthusiastic,
Like a bubbling glass of pop or soda,
They offer the highest quality of education.

Organization is her favourite tool,
Creative, concise, clear lesson plans,
Prepares students for their future endeavors,
Like a life coach she extrinsically motivates,
Language the essential tool of communication,
Their lessons enriches the classroom experience,
They meet each and every student's need,
A professional teacher is loved indeed!

A Natural Phenomenon
By: Kass Ghayouri

It played a game of hide and seek,
The body of water vanished,
Only to appear minutes later,
Like a gigantic, vindictive monster,
Monstrous, mauling, massive wall,
Headed straight for the shore.

The Killer Waves showed no mercy,
Roar, roar, roar it rushed in with rage,
With wild waves at 500 miles an hour,
It was just another passing jet plane,
It rose beyond... beyond 100 feet,
Like some mythical, maniac monster.

What psychological trauma it left behind,
Vulnerable victims with no hope,
Clinging desperately to any debris,
Trees uprooted and houses crashed,
Engulfing buildings and ripping vehicles,
It hungrily swallowed everything.

Men and women had to, "throw in the towel"
It was but a love hate relationship,
Over the miles they flew to enjoy its waters,
It's pulchritudinous water- a treacherous tyrant,
Billions of destitute, impecunious tourists,
Got much more than they bargained for.

Different Types of Poetry

Kass Ghayouri

Acrostic Poetry (Technology)
By: Kass Ghayouri

Transforms our present education,
Education becomes even more advanced,
Classroom is a glimpse into the future,
Happening so fast and furious,
Numerous, iPads, Smart phones and more,
Overwhelming use of electronics,
Learning integrates technology,
On Facebook we all socialize,
Grasping the computer as a tool,
YouTube used for demonstrations.

Acrostic Poetry (Computer)
By: Kass Ghayouri

Carries out different programs,
Operates to provide information,
Memory stored in a hard drive,
Powerful tool to research topics,
Unique, sophisticated machine,
Technology with integrated circuits,
Electronic Digital device is designed,
Readily stores infinite memory.

Acrostic Poetry (Facebook)
By: Kass Ghayouri

Facebook is a social networking service,
Adding international friendships,
Creating a social atmosphere,
Everyone's page is visible on your wall,
Blocking those obnoxious friends,
Outstanding pictures of social events,
Orchestrating a melody of friendships,
Keeping in touch with family and friends.

Cinquain (Natural Disasters)
By: Kass Ghayouri

Earthquake,
Point of rupture,
Shake, rupture, collapse, move,
Aftermath is devastating,
Earth's crust.

Twirling,
Tornado twirls,
Breaking, lifting, mauling,
Notoriously dividing
Swirling.

Wild waves,
Tsunami speeds,
Slashes, destroys, lashes,
Panic stricken people lost lives,
Ocean.

Thunder,
Lightning flashes,
Nears fiercely, rumbles, falls,
Thunderstorm keeps people housebound,
Hail storm.

SONNETS
By: Kass Ghayouri

LOVE
Love is the virtue of compassion,
Essence of love is the beat of my heart,
Transposed in a compassionate fashion.
Depressed when romantic love has to part,
Potent sentiment of being in love,
Reciprocating mutual feelings,
Identifying Gods gift from above,
With attachment and intimate dealings,
Intimacy is what makes lovers bond,
Love is a sensual desire of a longing,
Psychological view of being fond,
Loyal relationship of belonging,
Committed love is what I desire,
Romantic feelings of love is burning.

WAR
Yes the essence of war is destruction,
And the offensive force of repulsion,
Violent conflict requires construction,
Submission, survival and expulsion,
A phenomenon of serious warfare,
Fundamental existence of conflict,
Facing the antagonist if they dare,
Political control of the district,
Missile bombs and movement of the ground troop,
Then assassination and genocide,
A soldier treading as his shoulders droop,
Consequently a treaty to abide,
Potential destruction of a nation,
Tyrants control the vast population.

by Kass Chayouni

Social Issues

Black sheep of the family
By: Kass Ghayouri

And give it a shout,
The odd person out,
On gossip they thrive,
She can survive,
No need to fit in,
That is not a sin.

She does not pretend,
Her hearts contend,
To get into good books,
Why change your looks?
She speaks her mind,
One that's hard to find.

She knows the fact,
To limit such contact,
It's time to stay away,
What would the family say?
That is the black sheep,
They gossip and weep.

She's a beacon of light,
Gives an intelligent fight,
Knows how to succeed,
So intelligent indeed,
She rises to the top,
Black sheep does not stop.

Takes the leadership role,
Reaching the North Pole,
Changing her life style,
Going the extra mile,
Different form the rest,
Black sheep is the best.

Black Sheep…(continued)
By: Kass Ghayouri

Different from the clan,
She has her own plan,
Away from the family rally,
Walks up her lucky ally,
Has the recessive gene,
What does the idiom mean?

Black sheep in a flock of white,
Racism is just not right,
Heterozygous for black,
What trait does she lack?
That is a social norm,
When did this title form?

A racist derogative term,
The black sheep is a germ,
Devaluated by a family member,
Who is deviant...remember!
Unsuccessful and uneducated,
Jealous and finally ill fated.

The black sheep became a star,
Intellectually travelled far,
With higher social status,
Overcame all the gray status,
Achieved economic and social power,
Blossomed like a beautiful flower.

Now she stands so tall,
That team did not make her fall,
Proud of her achievement,
Despite the negative treatment,
The fairytale of the black sheep,
A success story that runs deep.

41

The Summer School Drama Queen
By: Kass Ghayouri

Trying to be in the lime light,
Ending up in an awkward plight,
Blowing information out of proportion,
Providing gossip with all distortion,
A melodramatic, narcissist attention seeker,
Thriving to make a situation weaker.

Wanting to be the centre of attention,
Often landing herself in detention,
Egocentric, entertaining, exciting personality type,
Neurotic personality where drama is ripe,
Explosive, emotional, exotic outburst,
Craving the spotlight with immense thirst.

Caring only about her personal needs,
A diva prone to exercising jealous deeds,
Her emotions like walking on egg shells,
Her persuasive powerful voice like church bells,
Histrionic tendencies reveal a drama queen,
A self-centered perfectionist prone to being mean.

Selfish, sarcastic, severe manipulative ways,
Projecting heat like the suns radiant rays,
Out of social and political loop,
Irrational when placed in a social group,
A drama queen does not earn trust,
Notoriously self-centered with triggered lust.

Drama Queen is a teacher's worst nightmare,
Uttering profanities with no care,
Changing the dynamics of the class,
Academically striving not to pass,
Not even motivated to succeed,
A personification of a pest indeed.

Her eyeballs roll form left to right,
Not hesitating to pick a fight,
Overlooking a teacher's command,
To take control upon immediate demand,
Like a dog the drama queen begins to bark,
The peaceful classroom atmosphere turns dark.

Loyalty
By: Kass Ghayouri

Thank you loyal friend,
For lending me your ear,
Listening to my problems,
When trouble rolls in,
As tears stream down,
You do not leave my side.

Deep dark secrets you hold,
Your unconditional love,
I get all your attention,
Feeling all the affection,
Your way of showing appreciation,
Thank you dear friend!

It's hard to find a loyal friend,
Who wipes away your tears,
One who makes you secure,
Protects you from danger,
Changes tears to laughter,
And your sadness to joy.

Puts their life on the line for you,
Never letting you down,
That's my loyal friend,
One I can always depend on,
Greets me at the door,
With such cheerful excitement.

Thank you loyal friend,
Your body language shows you care,
You do not walk away from me,
Accepting me as I am,
That's the friend of my dream,
A friend in need is a friend indeed!

Good Friends
By: Kass Ghayouri

Good Friends are hard to find,
Polite, thoughtful and kind,
Helps you when in trouble,
And does not have a double,
When you are in need,
That's a real friend indeed.

When you are in pain,
Walking down your lane,
It's that friend who will care,
That friend is so rare,
Giving you empathy,
Showing you sympathy.

Fighting all your battles,
Like a snake that rattles,
Venom is what they spit,
Until your enemy will split,
Putting their life on the line,
That friend is just so fine.

Does not talk behind your back,
This friend is first in your pack,
Always there to defend you,
Supports you in all that you do,
Never jealous about your life,
Maybe a husband or a wife.

Appreciation is what they show,
Love for them will always grow,
Will always take your side,
In this friend you can confide,
Never uses you for money,
Always witty and so funny.

Gossip
By: Kass Ghayouri

Personal and private affair,
By someone who does not care,
Engaging in idle talk,
Delivers gossip like a stalk,
A reputation down the drain,
Then tears flow down like rain,
Gossiping to friends and strangers,
Not considering the dangers,
Like butter he spreads the dirt,
Gossip causes so much hurt,
About social and personal life,
A friend, mother, sibling and wife,
Delights in such idle tattle,
With inner demons he has to battle,
How do I rise above such gossip?
And try to keep a tight lip,
It is a form of verbal attack,
As soon as I turn my back,
He tries to gain control and power,
Gossiping to friends by the hour,
Like the courier he delivers his tale,
Gossip delivered like an open mail,
His low self-esteem comes into play,
People listen to what he has to say,
Enhancing his social prestige,
Friends' attention he will siege,
Gossip spread through the grapevine,
Malicious gossip is just not fine,
Gossip that's intellectually unproductive,
In a style that's intimately seductive,
Gossip with a domestic scope,
Acting as innocent as the Pope,
Demeans the dignity of such a man,
The listener has to be the fan,
The evil tongue lashes out,

Domestic affairs is what it's about,
Religion views gossip as a sin,
An empty vessel makes all the din,
Victims hurt by such backbiting,
Leads to uncountable fighting,
Victims left with no chance of defense,
Malicious gossip does not make sense,
It's like eating a victim's flesh,
Needs protection with an iron mesh,
Resolve disputes with the person in mind,
A true friend is hard to find,
Conflict resolution is a real need,
That's unrighteous, wicked gossip indeed,
The feelings of separateness is rife,
Living with a gossiper is a negative life,
It brings the victim such shame,
The gossip monger has to take the blame,
It leads to such emotional harm,
Maintaining a personality that's calm,
What the gossiper wishes to gain,
Is he normal or is he insane?
It is so easy to lose trust,
Communication is definitely a must,
A gossip manager trying to clear the name,
Gossip becomes a dangerous game,
When the gossip reaches its end,
It's the broken heart the victim will mend.

Dance Mania
By: Kass Ghayouri

The couple enters at the door,
Rhythmically steps onto the floor,
Motion from the left to the right,
Erotic movements though the night,
Moving to the rhythm of the beat,
Ecstatic movement of the feet,
Interpretive movement of the bop,
Disco, tango, waltz, and hip hop,
Listening to the music soar,
The electronic sound begins to roar,
Such collective ecstasy as they wind,
Regenerating music in their mind,
Dancing until they hit their peak,
Moving like a psychedelic freak,
The phenomenon of a unique sound,
Seamless movements on the ground,
Embracing the elements of the song,
A club where nothing can go wrong,
Disco takes the floor by storm,
A variety of style, format and form,
Highly choreographed and driven beat,
Strobe lights brings about the heat,
Hands begin to revolve around,
The hip and pelvis move to the sound,
Graciously steps forward and then back,
Shoulders tilt and then become slack,
Repetitive steps induce a trance,
Music raves as the couple continues to dance.

Moral Values
By: Kass Ghayouri

Oversized and so tall,
Moral values take a fall,
His poor ethnical values,
His personality devalues,
Lacks respect for adults,
Indulges in verbal insults.

Diminish the power of authority,
He has no sense of morality,
No honesty, integrity, or compassion,
Disrespect in an unethical fashion,
He has negative character traits,
Like a bully he dictates.

Raised like Frankenstein,
Loves to complain and whine,
With manipulative control,
He plays the victim's role,
Gossiping to get attention,
The school gives him suspension.

Frankenstein's creator spoils,
In fear the monster recoils,
Not taught what's right or wrong,
Oversized but not strong,
Cries to get attention from others,
With attention his creator smothers.

Teachers show him apathy,
His creator gives him empathy,
He finds it difficult to read,
He has little education indeed,
Furthermore he cannot write,
With teachers he displays fright.

Table Manners
By: Kass Ghayouri

An insatiable appetite,
Greed with each bite,
Cannot share a group meal,
Obesity is not a big deal,
Parent does not really track,
On the unhealthy snack,
The adolescent is obese,
The eating does not cease,
The parent does not control,
Playing a submissive role,
Allows the child to dominate,
Overloading the dinner plate,
Gobbles a meal for four,
Greedily asking for more,
Diabetes and hypertension,
No lifestyle intervention,
Complex maladaptive behaviour,
The adolescent needs a savior,
Degree of rapidly, rising rate,
Obesity and overweight,
No parental responsibility,
Discipline is a possibility,
No limit on his portion size,
He targets food as his prize,
Table manners he lacks,
Self-Indulgent food he stacks,
Hastily gobbles like in a race,
Eating at an incredible pace,
Leaving little for others to eat,
Table manners are not discreet.

Sari
By: Kass Ghayouri

A garment with a flow,
Sitting on the hips so low,
Six meters in length,
A fabric with strength,
Wrapped around the waist,
You cannot tie in haste,
With elegance and grace,
Worn by the Indian race,
An amazing attire,
Various styles to admire,
Draped in different ways,
Elegantly it always stays,
So beautiful and bright,
So graceful and light,
Worn with a short blouse,
Outside and in the house,
Pleats like a flower,
Styles one would endower,
Over the right shoulder,
With a pin jewel holder,
A royal fashion repertoire,
An Indian woman wore,
Gorgeous beautiful drape,
Over the body like a cape,
Embroidery of rich gold,
Beads and patterns so bold,
A fashionable trend,
With a colorful blend,
It has its sex appeal,
It's an amazing deal,
Like an evening dress,
The body it will caress.

Psychological
Issues

Trust
By: Kass Ghayouri

Ashes to ashes,
Dust to dust,
Mourn the death of trust,
It's easy to lose,
It's hard to gain,
How can you ever trust again?

To trust or not trust,
What's your perception?
After such deception,
When trust is violated,
You have been betrayed,
Distrust is portrayed.

To forgive or not to forgive,
Gossiping is disrespect,
Trust is what you expect,
Takes time to rebuild trust,
The perpetrator causes you grief,
How do you gain any relief?

You try to restore trust,
Healing takes time,
Those stairs to climb,
Trust can be rebuilt,
Trust in a friendship,
Trust in a partnership.

Personality Clashes
By: Kass Ghayouri

With those you bond,
Become really fond,
Others you despise,
With all their white lies,
Then the bully appears,
Brings you nothing but tears.

The one with the mood,
Often blunt and rude,
The one that's naïve,
You wish they would leave,
One who would backstab,
Your attention they grab.

The one who knows all,
Don't take their phone call,
One that loves to boast,
Is the one you hate the most,
The one that is stern,
Makes your stomach churn.

The one with charm,
Brings you no harm,
A friend who is loyal,
That's a friend that's royal,
One who speaks straight,
That friend is so great.

The one with the big mouth,
You don't want to clout,
She will speak her mind,
A friend that's hard to find,
What personality traits!
You find in your mates.

Emotions
By: Kass Ghayouri

Happiness is synonymous of cheerful,
Bubbly, buoyant, content, and gleeful,
Effervescing, ecstatic, euphoric and delighted,
Glad, jolly, jovial, jubilant and excited,
It places you in a vibrant, vivacious place,
Forming a harmonious, optimistic base.

Sadness is synonymous of dejected,
Depressed, desolate, dismal and rejected,
Forlorn, gloomy, glum, somber and distraught,
Perturbed, pessimistic, poignant and taut,
You are melancholic, solemn with disgrace,
Wretched, heartbroken problems to face.

Madness is synonymous of frantic,
Aggravated, berserk, delirious, and frenetic,
Fuming, infuriated, livid, and frustrated,
Seething, vicious, violent, and exasperated,
You find yourself in an irate, raging case,
Forming a riled, enraged, incensed race.

Shyness is synonymous for skittish,
Apprehensive, bashful, cloistered, and sheepish,
Demure, docile, embarrassed, and meek,
Hesitant, introverted, modest and weak,
You form a solitary, submissive, wary lace,
Moving at an infusive, self-conscious pace.

Love is definitely synonymous of affectionate,
Amorous, ardor, consideration and adulate,
Exalt, fancy, fondness, tenderness and dedication,
Cherish, empathy, esteem, and devotion,
You can show passion and honor with ace,
Placing someone in a treasured, valued place.

Hate is synonymous of animosity,
Abominate, contempt, dislike and hostility,
Antagonism, deride, detest and bitterness,
Loathing, malice, rancor and wickedness,
You can show resent to any race,
That is spiteful and even a disgrace.

Worried is synonymous of tense,
Anxious, apprehensive, edgy and dense,
Bothered, distressed, fretful and distraught,
Nervous, overwhelmed, perturbed, and taut.
You can display vexed feelings in any place,
All stemming from having a plagued place.

Poisoned Potion
By: Kass Ghayouri

He poisoned her heart with love,
He poisoned her mind with hate,
He poisoned her drink with seeds,
He poisoned her friends with gossip,
He poisoned her family with threats,
He poisoned her life with kindness.

He poisoned the child with affection,
He poisoned his friends with attention,
He poisoned his family with appreciation,
He poisoned his sibling with money,
He poisoned his uncle with loyalty,
He poisoned her with his wealth.

She was poisoned by his mere devotion,
She was poisoned by his brutal honesty,
She was poisoned by his physical appearance,
She was poisoned by his sense of purity,
She was poisoned by his loyal service,
She was poisoned by his sincere dedication.

She was poisoned by his good manners,
She was poisoned by his lack of communication,
She was poisoned by his physical presence,
She was poisoned by his sense of purity,
She was poisoned by his loyal service,
She was poisoned by his sincere dedication.

Poison entered into her blood stream,
Poison caused her immense pain,
Poison hospitalized her for months,
Poison brought death knocking at her door,
Poison alerted spiritual intervention,
Poison did not know she was immortal!

Histrionics
By: Kass Ghayouri

Her life's a hyperbole!
Often so exaggerated,
A personality disorder,
Outrageous emotional behaviour,
With such social realms.

Often loud and so dramatic,
Borderline personality disorder,
Scanning out the room,
Like a rodent she creeps,
In search of a dramatic clique.

Impulsivity and over activity,
With each shot for alcoholic beverage,
The dramatic monologue begins,
Like thunder her laughter roars,
Like an eagle her voice soars.

Sarcastic with dramatic irony,
The amateur theatrical antics,
In search of an instant fan club,
Animated facial expression,
Melancholic body language.

Focus exclusively on her,
She is portrayed as shallow,
She becomes sexually seductive,
Her provocative behaviour exposed,
Manipulative and in control.

A threat to family and friends,
Depressed with no attention,
Becomes the queen of the show,
She craves novelty stimulation,
Deviates from her routine.

Wants immediate satisfaction,
Does not tolerate delayed gratification,
Indulges in impulse control,
Shallow expression of emotions,
Speaks excessively impressionistic.

Lacking in intelligence,
Easily influenced by others,
Histrionic personality disorder,
Hopefully decreases with age,
A great impact on her life.

Causation is bio psychosocial,
Inter wined with nature,
Biological and genetic cause,
Dramatic when copying with stress,
The drama queen lives on!

Referring to others affectionately,
Darling, Dear, Honey, Love!
Flirting with the opposite sex,
Engaging in sexual touch,
Seductive and inviting look!

Inappropriate dressing trend,
Wanting expensive gifts,
Aiming for monetary gain,
Unable to remain faithful,
Engaging in affairs of lust.

No intellectual conversation,
Engaging in perverted jokes,
No compassion for other's feelings,
Cunning and so manipulative,
Neglecting children and family ties!

Emotional Pain
By: Kass Ghayouri

Such emotional trauma,
Intense emotional pain,
Life becomes a dilemma,
Equilibrium is hard to gain,
The force of life is blocked,
Our world is finally locked,

The wound is raw,
We have to bury the feeling,
It is difficult to find the core,
The wound is not healing,
What really went wrong?
The hurt is painfully strong.

It is so difficult to survive,
Feelings of powerlessness and suffering,
Our psycho we need to revive,
Caught in a traumatic ring,
The vibrations of emotional pain,
Like a muscle with a sprain.

Threshold of pain by the hour,
Our energy we cannot align,
We can turn to the higher power,
A pain we just cannot define,
Feelings of rage, sadness and despair,
Apathy...as nobody will care!

A counselor is what we need,
In a whirlpool emotions spin,
To deal with the pain indeed,
Physically we grown so thin,
Pain like a tight constriction,
Such an emotional conviction.

The Power of Silence
By: Kass Ghayouri

When emotionally upset,
Your voice goes on strike,
Cannot articulate pain,
No verbal arguments,
You give the cold shoulder,
And the other feels the pain.

It is the sounds of silence,
Words not shed like bullets,
Tears not shed like the rain,
Being ignored is what hurts,
The pain of being treated like dirt,
It is the power of silence!

You have nothing to really say,
Silence ruins his entire day,
Walking past each other like strangers,
Glances are not exchanged,
The beginning of a cold war,
Your voice takes a leave of absence.

Emotionally you feel the bitter rage,
Your mind rewinds several times,
Your recall the problem that occurred,
The mind drifts like a dandelion,
From place to place, problem to problem,
Like a visual side in your head.

It is the power of silence,
Where you make the point,
A time of intense meditation,
Where your voice goes on strike,
Days, weeks, and maybe months,
Waiting patiently to break the ice.

Paradise on Wheels
By: Kass Ghayouri

Intensity of speed,
Wanting to be free,
In total control,
Leaving behind trouble,
Life can be great.

Riding on the bike,
Into the sunset,
Cutting through the air,
Like a skate on ice,
Hell's angels move on.

Like a rollercoaster ride,
Paradise on wheels,
Pleasure and no pain,
Freedom without restrain,
Zoom zoom zoom zoom!

Wind combs the hair,
A bird without feathers,
Flight without wings,
No care in the world,
Life in fast-forward.

A symbol of freedom,
The adrenalin rush,
What a mean machine,
Propels them forward,
Not rewinding the past.

Weaving through traffic,
Winding through bends,
Meandering through crowds,
Spinning on two wheels,
Has to be heaven on earth.

Life with a Sociopath
By: Kass Ghayouri

You were placed in a cold cell,
Burning beyond the gates of hell,
Cut out from all family ties,
Living a life of deception and lies,
The devil sneaked into your life,
Playing the role of a dutiful wife,
You were branded by her name,
She played the vicious game,
Labeled anything in her sight,
Then it was time for fight and flight,
A notorious fugitive on the run,
In search of a life full of fun,
With no cognitive perception,
Her character armed with deception,
Treated you as sweet as honey,
Yet had the claws on your money,
The responsibility of a mother,
A dedicated and dutiful father,
Amazing and precious children in tow,
She became the enemy and foe,
It's time to remove the shackle,
Life's sorrows you have to tackle,
Another evil and cunning plan,
She has duped another man,
Two amazing families torn apart,
Left stranded with a broken heart,
The histrionic personality type,
Sociopathic tendencies are ripe,
Lack of remorse and even shame,
Pathologic egocentricity to blame,
Willing to hurt others to achieve a goal,
Playing the likable and charming role.

A radiation of sexuality,
Manipulative and full of vitality,
Uncomfortable with those who are strong,
Violent outburst when all goes wrong,
Narcissistic and behaving superior,
Tactics to make others so inferior,
Inability to make eye contact,
Trying to mooch of others is a fact,
Each phrase with a profanity,
Egocentric and full of vanity,
A gold digger right from the start,
A woman with a malicious heart,
That psychopathic personality trait,
Irritability, aggressiveness with hate,
Conning others for profit and pleasure,
Infidelity as an act of leisure,
Insincerity and superficial charm,
Antisocial behaviour brings others harm,
Others around have to beware,
Because a sociopath does not care,
Hypnotic behaviour captures others attention,
Delusions of grandeur, great to mention,
A great orator with a fabricated story,
Confidence and assertiveness in all glory,
Others intoxicated by the charm,
Feeling no remorse, brings about harm,
Life has given you the big test,
A lesson from life is the best,
By a sociopath you were victimized,
Yet now you are truly victim-wise,
Stabbed you in the back with a knife,
God now hands you a PH D in life!

Motivation
(Poems)

Fortuneteller
By: Kass Ghayouri

Clairvoyant channels her inner voice,
Who comes through is not her choice,
Spirits of the dead are there to speak,
The truth makes you want to freak,
Describing your future and recalling the past,
Who knows what spell she can cast.

Tarot cards placed in a row,
A picture of a dagger and a crow,
Symbolic of death is what she saw,
Information so blunt and so raw,
Your future looks so bright and tense,
Whatever she says makes a lot of sense.

You have to drink all the black tea,
In the leaves your future she can see,
She sees an eagle that's in flight,
Meaning the future will be bright,
She names the friend and the foe,
Abundance of happiness and the end of woe.

Clairvoyant's clear clean crystal ball,
Your past and future she can recall,
Information makes you jump out of your skin,
Describing your future and next of kin,
She then goes into a deep trance,
You see your future at a glance.

Bestowed upon her a special gift,
Any evil spell she is able to lift,
Calling upon the spirits of the dead,
Your past and future is then read,
Revealing her special psychic power,
Such memories she has to endower.

Pull out the Plug!
By: Kass Ghayouri

You generously give,
They greedily take,
You show respect,
They do not appreciate,
Help them with schoolwork,
They take advantage,
You do so many favors,
They come back for more,
You feel obliged,
They expect much more,
Take you for granted,
You continue to be kind,
You call them friends,
Offer them hospitality,
Show no consideration,
Friends that use you,
Call you when they're in need,
Ignore you when not needed,
A one-way friendship,
Gossip behind your back,
That pushes your buttons,
Boundaries are crossed,
Friendships on eggshells,
Unspoken resentment,
Your inner dialogue,
Go with your instinct,
Their negative energy
Such catastrophe,
Pull out the plug!
Goodbye to a friendship,
Where you were used
And often abused.
Pull out the plug!

Follow Your Dreams!
By: Kass Ghayouri

Let no one put you down,
Your success makes them frown,
Reach for the blue sky,
Aim at going so high,
You need to be positive,
Avoid those who are negative.

If you feel it is right,
To see a future that's bright,
Set yourself that goal,
And adopt that successful role,
Strive to do your very best,
Do not worry about the rest.

You have to follow your dream,
Like a fast flowing stream,
There is no time to think,
Life vanishes with a blink,
Focus, Fantasize, frame your mind,
Abundance of success you will find.

Negative in every other way,
Do not listen to what they say,
A simple life is what you need,
Jealousy is what they breed,
Avoid the blockage in your path,
Envy, jealousy and negative wrath.

On cloud nine you can float,
About your success you can gloat,
You worked hard to follow that dream,
On you that spotlight will beam,
Abundance of wealth flows your way,
A star is born on an auspicious day.

Talent runs so Deep!
By: Kass Ghayouri

It's not time to say goodbye,
Oh no I will not die,
My future holds success,
I am not settling for less,
At the end of my rainbow,
Is a pot of gold lying low.

My mission is not complete,
My life you cannot delete,
The devil lies beneath your soul,
Placing you in a deep, dark hole,
Influenced and duped by another,
An evil foe, a sister or a brother.

I am not a fool but wise,
Stand back and watch me rise,
I do not need your permission,
To gracefully conquer my mission,
Do not staple me to the ground,
Watch my success come around.

Like an eagle I will soar,
Opening up that heavenly door,
Like a vulture I will claw,
Maintaining perfection not a flaw,
Like an owl I am wise,
Using education to rise.

Together we can work as a team,
Reaching out for that dream,
All that knowledge to share,
For those opportunists beware!
Hard work with little sleep,
My talent runs so deep.

Cheerleader
By: Kass Ghayouri

We all need a cheerleader,
When you're feeling depressed,
Immediately they cheer you up,
When you achieve success,
They dance, jump, and cheer,
When you make a big win,
They promote a joyful spirit,
When an enemy suddenly attacks,
They will stunt and then boo,
When you take a sudden fall
Cheerleading can then endure,
When you feel intense moods,
You cheerleader dances with you,
When you are feeling stress,
Your cheerleader motivates you,
When you experience failure,
They take pride to lead you,
When you feel isolated,
Your cheerleader is your biggest fan,
When you go up in life,
Your cheerleader shows off your spirit,
When your health declines,
Your cheerleader is your support,
When you cannot pursue,
Your cheerleader encourages you,
Your cheerleader has no glitter,
Has no pom poms or face paint,
Your cheerleader is your husband,
Your cheerleader is your wife,
A friend, a mother or a father,
That cheers you on in life!

Aging
By: Kass Ghayouri

Aging is like a natural disaster,
Your cholesterol is like a tsunami,
Rolling in with massive waves,
Your diabetes is like a tornado,
Chronic condition of swirling insulin,
Your stress is like a hurricane,
With fierce winds and tears like rain,
Your blood pressure is like a landslide,
Collapses and slides downward,
Your thyroid is like an avalanche,
Turbulent, hazardous current moves down,
Your mood is like a volcanic eruption,
Releasing poisonous gasses and eruptions,
Your menopause is like a wildfire,
Producing ember attacks and threats,
Your digestive system is like a drought,
Severe deficiency of its water supply,
Your heartbeat is like an earthquake,
Creating seismic waves and tremors,
Your arthritis is like a snowstorm,
With cold weather you shovel the pain,
Your memory is like a massive flood,
Thoughts like water flow outside the brain,
Your headache is like a thunderstorm,
Pounding with loud obnoxious sounds,
Cancer is like intense lightening,
It hits you so suddenly with one strike,
Aging is like a natural disaster,
Even doctors cannot predict,
What disasters nature may bring!

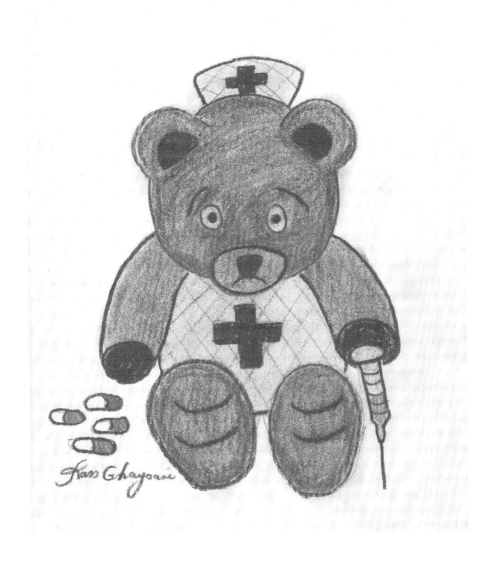

You have Male!
By: Kass Ghayouri

Yes, you have male!
Received by the female,
A package in your mailbox,
As sly as a male fox,
Arrives from another planet,
Attracted like a magnet.

The sender is his mother,
Yes, made by no other,
Retreats into his cave,
Another emotional wave,
It's "time-out" from life,
Runs away from his wife.

The female wants to talk,
However, he takes a walk,
To get a new perspective,
With her he cannot live,
He then wants to leave,
Leaving her to grieve.

The male begins to retreat,
The female feels defeat,
A woman needs attention,
He puts her in detention,
Withdrawing his affection,
Giving no appreciation!

Problems in the relationship,
Man and woman lose the grip,
No talent and no gift,
Her spirit he cannot lift,
He shows no gratitude,
With his obnoxious attitude.

Anger, sadness and fear,
Not having him near,
Support is what she deserves,
He gives her weak nerves,
Pain of being rejected,
With one button she's ejected.

He wants to be needed,
Problems have to be weeded,
He wants to feel support,
To whom does he report?
Mistress or concubine,
To whom he can whine.

Abundance of love to give,
For the relationship to live,
Differences to explore,
And children to adore,
New understanding of men,
New definition of women.

Resentment comes to an end,
The marriage has to mend,
Increase mutual trust,
Forgiveness has to be a "must"
You cannot return to sender,
That will make you an offender!

Right from Wrong!
By: Kass Ghayouri

Who's right and wrong?
It's the age-old song,
An argument or a fight,
Who is really right?
Who do we blame?
The problem is so lame.

Nobody is perfect,
We all have a defect,
We try to defend,
We need to amend,
To repair the damage,
To create an image.

We try to see their side,
In friends we confide,
Angry insults hurt,
Revealing all the dirt,
A fight that's not civil,
An argument that's evil.

A game of revenge,
One tries to avenge,
Who do we punish?
Who is really selfish?
To compromise,
Have to be wise.

To repair the rupture,
Our ego we capture,
Modeling forgiveness,
Trying to be selfless,
There is no right and wrong,
Those words are strong!

Shopping
By: Kass Ghayouri

Shopping sets the mood,
So often misunderstood,
Psychological Therapy,
Women shop happily,
It removes their stress,
A cognitive process.

All those designer brands,
Shopping bags in her hands,
Those fashionable trends,
Depressing mood it mends,
She is so happy to browse,
Her interest will arouse.

You know how she feels,
With those amazing deals,
She knows how to spend,
Latest clothing trend,
Satisfying her emotional need,
She is relaxed indeed.

Men do not understand,
The expression, "Cash in hand,"
Successful woman's money,
She works so hard, honey!
Shopping in the mall,
Economic status will not fall.

Removes her emotional pain,
Confident and even vain,
Meander through the malls,
Through clothing she sprawls,
Shopping is her mission,
She does not need his permission.

Detoxification
By: Kass Ghayouri

Removing toxins,
A cleanse for life,
Cleansing your mind,
Of those toxic friends,
Follow that gut feeling,
She is the opportunist.

They prey on you,
And your materialistic assets,
They lack theory of the mind,
With no logical thinking,
Only accepting their point of view,
Unable to provide a reason.

It's time to detach,
It's time to ditch them,
Providing a fake friendship,
Jealous of your success,
A poisonous friendship,
You are just their therapist.

They call when they need help,
They call to use you,
They draw on your energy,
It's time to cut that bond,
Of that one sided friendship.

Time to distance yourself,
You need to create boundaries,
They reveal disrespect,
Detoxification it is,
It's time to say goodbye!

Sports

Soccer
By: Kass Ghayouri

Teammates to pick,
A soccer ball to kick,
Run across the field,
Then suddenly they yield,
To score a special goal,
Playing a talented role,
Elements of the soccer game,
Scoring brings them fame,
Opponents don't play fair,
Playing foul if they dare,
No physical contact allowed,
The fans cheers out aloud,
Teams with most goals win,
The crowd makes a loud din,
A few fixed dimensions,
With animated actions,
Colors that distinguish a jersey,
Team players strong and burly,
A team player shoots the pass,
Players run across the grass,
They need to shield the ball,
"Foul" the referee can call,
Each team has its tactics,
Cheered by lots of fanatics,
With momentum and speed,
They pounce just to succeed,
Jump into the air and head,
Amongst the defenders they spread,
Under pressure and anticipation,
Crowds scream in frustration,
It's time to celebrate,
As the cheers escalate.

Basketball
By: Kass Ghayouri

Running and passing,
Shooting and dribbling,
Tall like a giraffe,
The players defend,
Weakening the defense,
Like a lion with its prey.

Players are sliding ice skaters,
Like a thief he steals the ball,
He moves in for the shot,
As the other shades his face,
Thin, tall, tough players,
Jump like hopping kangaroos.

A player fakes a pump,
As the other tries to jump,
The other knocks the ball,
As if staging an accident,
They take every risk,
Like gambling at a casino.

Chances of making a hook,
Following rules by the book,
Hands up like a police arrest,
Blocking a pass and a shot,
Using all peripheral vision,
Tracking the balls movement.

It's a bitter sweet moment,
Trying to trick the opponent,
Like a magician with his tricks,
Gives birth to defense specialists,
Moving through the court,
Dedication to the game.

Karate
By: Kass Ghayouri

Delivering a block,
Getting an arm lock,
Delivering a blow,
Head dives really low,
Performing bare foot,
Giving an owls hoot,
The belt shows the skill,
The opponent is still,
Clothing is padded,
Colored belt is added,
Japanese martial art,
Attacking a body part,
Players start fighting,
Moving like lightening,
Lots of self-defense,
The movements are dense,
Powerful linear technique,
Making the opponent weak,
Taking deep strong stances,
The opponent dances,
With physical movement,
And mental improvement,
Based on perfect thinking,
Concentrate and no blinking,
Player with an open mind,
The right movement to find,
A tribute to Bruce Lee,
He was powerful and free,
Bow as a symbol of respect,
Self-control and intellect.

Spiritual
Poems

A Metaphoric Garbage Can
By: Kass Ghayouri

You are that garbage can,
A personification of junk,
Gobbling flavored fast food,
Sodas, sugar, salt, savories,
Dumping garbage through your mouth,
Your mouth is symbolic of a garbage can.

Disgusting discarded animal matter,
Becomes trash in your mouth,
Fried, cooked, roasted, animal carcass
Becomes waste in your body,
Garbage is placed in waste bins,
Not sent through your mouth.

You leave your body to recycle,
That bloated tummy your landfill,
Extends with heaped compost,
With junk food and fast food,
Consumption of such waste,
Oral disposing of waste products.

It is called waste management,
Significant health justice issue,
The human body exposed to junk food,
Just like the over flowing garbage can,
Your body begins to decay,
Food in every nook and cranny.

The world is eating itself to death,
The organs begin to disfunction,
Diabetes and high blood pressure,
From a garbage can to a landfill,
You extend in size and weight,
Think, thrive, and then totally treat!

Why does Formal Education take so Long?
By: Kass Ghayouri

From grade one to eight,
Education moves at a slow rate,
From grade nine to twelve,
On theories we have to delve,
Four years of university,
Subjects with so much diversity.

Honors, Masters, and P.H.D,
Finally from studies we are free,
It takes time to get education,
Then a vocational occupation,
Why does education have to take time?
Developing wisdom without spending a dime.

Need for formal institutional instruction,
Without it will there be utter destruction?
Does wisdom have to come with age?
Do we have to follow each educational stage?
Acknowledging education by a grade,
Teacher's biases and judgments are made.

Education should not be determined by time,
Parents, educators, teachers, leaders are prime,
Students with degrees are unemployed,
Unsuccessful, unlucky, poor and annoyed,
An uneducated singer with talent on the street,
Making millions with hysterical fans to greet!

Aptitude is a component of talent,
Brings about success that's innovative or violent,
Spiritual teaching of consciousness is the core,
Insightful teaching that opens up another door,
Formal education may enslave humanity,
Conscious evolution that brings about vanity.

We all have a talent to share in life,
Conscious powerful cosmic change is rife,
Nurture and nature, a child's aptitude from birth,
A successful duty they can perform on Earth,
Free us from the traditional teaching,
Humanity guided towards comprehensive preaching.

I am a Poet
By: Kass Ghayouri

My poetry is not from my mind,
My poetry emerges from my soul,
It brings with it a message,
It gives voice to my soul,
A voice that hopes to inspire,
And inspires you to listen!

The highest degree of wisdom,
Escapes through my poetry,
Expressed with loyal passion,
Written with logical reasoning,
The neocortex of my brain,
Is a personification of reasoning!

My skillful knowledge and virtue,
Delivered to you in images and words,
Poetry a personification of a mail man,
Receiving the acquisition of knowledge,
That helps you realize your value in life,
Poetry is my knowledge and experience!

My poetry emerges with sincerity,
It's my ethical beliefs and advice,
The ability to enhance my insight,
As a teacher I share knowledge,
As a poet I demonstrate wisdom,
Cognitive, emotional and spiritual advice!

My poems emerge with powerful emotions,
With a rhythm that makes you chant,
My poems deliver powerful words,
That inspires you to rap or to rant,
Words echoed from my spiritual soul,
Enables me to generously share!

My Spiritual Mind
By: Kass Ghayouri

My mind is my home,
A place that I occupy,
My permanent residence,
A place where I belong,
My ideas and attitudes,
Reside in my mind.

My mind is a spiritual home,
My mind is my heaven,
A home with positive cleansing,
A home embedded with love,
Perception occupies my mind,
I perceive what's outside to find.

My thoughts are my guest,
I invite into my home,
I eliminate obnoxious guests,
I invite guests that are pure,
Obnoxious guests bring me pain,
My mind, my home, a place of rest.

My front door is my middle eye,
A door to higher consciousness,
Invites spiritual and mental images,
Brings positive aura to my home,
Leads me to my pineal gland,
My mystic mind I call my home.

My spiritual mind is free of worries,
A home free of anxiety and fear,
My symbol of strength and power,
My thoughts a united harmonious family,
My mind is liberated and elevated,
My mind is my luxurious mansion!

Manifestation of Thoughts
By: Kass Ghayouri

Thoughts become reality,
Life then becomes vitality,
You knowingly attract,
You need to retract,
Attract what you desire,
Thoughts that you admire.
It is all that you think,
The universe will link,
It is all about attraction,
Thoughts bring satisfaction,
Visualize what you need,
You plant that futile seed.
A desire in your mind,
What joy you will find,
On a thought you dwell,
The universe you will tell,
It is all that you dream,
And what you would redeem.
Your desires will come true,
The universe presents a clue,
To the universe you send a fax,
Then lay back and relax,
Abundance is what it will create,
Attraction of good luck and fate.
Negative energy can be strong,
That's when everything goes wrong,
Positive energy brings peace,
All the burdens that you release,
Manifestation of your thought,
Good luck is what it brought.

Rass Ghayouri

Be a Warrior
By: Kass Ghayouri

You need to be a warrior,
And go on an adventure,
Do not let time slow you down,
Display your own courage,
Maintain your faith and loyalty,
Value and honor yourself.

You are your very own hero,
Display vigor, vitality and strength,
Go out there and conquer the world,
With intellectual and athletic traits,
You control your own destiny,
Put an end to your worries and fear.

The universe is your loyal friend,
It showers you with wealth,
Your journey of self-discovery,
Win the battle over your demons,
Reveal yourself with noble honor,
Strive, sacrifice and succeed.

You have one battle to fight,
Destroying your negative energy,
Go on that adventurous journey,
To excel in what you are good at,
Seek to make amends in your world,
With success you find honor.

When our adventure comes to an end,
You have attained tranquility,
Filled with wisdom, truth and strength,
A foundation of ethical values,
You are the brave and successful warrior,
An adventure that brought you honor.

Spiritual Morals
By: Kass Ghayouri

Vow to abstain,
From evil actions,
Ethical conduct,
Positive attainment,
Practice non violence,
Promote love and peace.

Respect the living,
Point of conception,
The cycle of life,
Sanctity of life,
It's enlightenment,
Protection of life.

Ethical conversation,
Moral code of conduct,
No destruction of life,
Control gluttony,
The act of craving,
Act of compassion.

Its vegetarianism,
Ethics of killing,
For the sake of consumption,
The karmic desires,
The act of parity,
Spiritual dedication.

I am...
By: Kass Ghayouri

I am the eye,
Providing spiritual sight,
I am the sun,
Bringing ultimate power,
I am the angel,
A symbol of good protection,
I am the arrow,
A positive direction,
I am a butterfly,
The soul of new creation,
I am the circle,
I bring you wholeness,
I am the bull,
My mythical duality,
I am the compass,
Moving towards perfection,
I am a cow,
A symbol of enlightenment,
I am the crescent,
My victory over death,
I am the eagle,
Symbolic of victory,
I am the dove,
I bring about peace,
I am the dragon,
Embracing the spiritual force,
I am fire,
Always shining bright,
I am a fish,
Bringing good luck,
I am a lion,
The strength of power,
I am a spiritual symbol.

Meditation
By: Kass Ghayouri

All about dedication,
It's intense meditation,
To train the mind,
Relaxation to find,
A religious belief,
A spiritual relief,
A self regulation,
Sustained by concentration,
Mantras can be chanted,
Prayers taken for granted,
Ritual beads to keep track,
Anger and hatred to lack,
It's a state of calm,
Can bring you no harm,
A specific mental style,
Concentration for a while,
Familiar with the self,
Like a book on a shelf,
Spiritual practice of Buddhism,
Mantras chanted in Hinduism,
To spiritually contemplate,
To calmly sit and meditate,
In every religious tradition,
Prayer in the form of meditation,
Desirable light of the divine,
A higher state to incline,
Repetition of a religious phrase,
A spiritual and secular daze,
Across cultures and traditions,
The practice of meditation.

Spiritual Enlightenment
By: Kass Ghayouri

Your personal perception,
Your very own conception,
Your thoughts are positive,
You do not think negative,
A new way of thinking,
New concepts you linking.

Individual self portrays,
All negativity frays,
A new form of action,
A religious interaction,
You are now so content,
Your thoughts are not bent.

A journey of awakening,
A ritual is overtaking,
Pay attention to health,
Attract happiness and wealth,
A form of self realization,
The benefits of meditation.

Clearing your inner mind,
Peace you would find,
Mind, body, and soul,
Reached a spiritual whole,
It is time to really heal,
A balance of mind you feel.

Symbolic Awareness
By: Kass Ghayouri

The lizard creeps,
Your souls awareness,
The mask is worn,
Our ancestral spirits,
The mermaid swims,
She guards your treasures,
The owl observes,
Bringing you wisdom,
The phoenix is the sun,
Resurrection and immortality,
The snake slithers,
Representing temptation,
The spider spins,
It spins a fate of good luck,
The sun spreads its rays,
It is the cosmic womb,
Stick out that tongue,
Your flame, fire, and fertility,
Carving that totem,
Ancestral spiritual power,
Symbol of that unicorn,
A renewal of eternal life,
Observe that wheel,
It's our circle of life,
Ever snapped that wishbone,
Your dreams come true,
The yin yang the universal symbol,
Brings one balance and harmony,
The frog hops in,
Bringing healing and prosperity,
Sharing the message,
Of symbolic awareness.

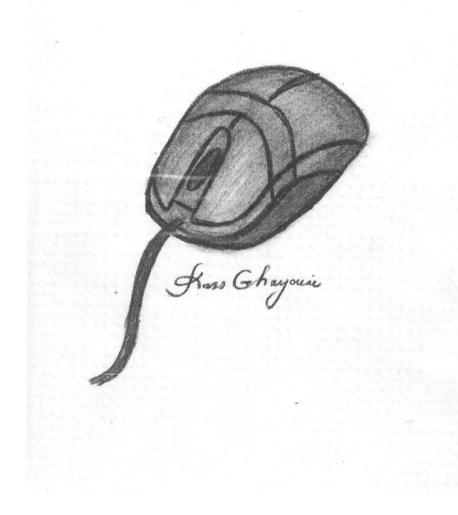

Dreams
By: Kass Ghayouri

Narrative and concrete,
Nightmarish with defeat,
The nature of each dream,
Comes with an interesting theme,
With such impulsive thought,
Is what the dream brought.
Recalling at a conscious level,
Conflict from an angel or devil,
A dream full of restlessness,
Recalled during wakefulness,
It's symbols of the past,
Dreams of memories that last.
A psychoanalytic tradition,
A psychological interpretation,
Dreaming of a future event,
Logical thinking that's bent,
The impossible in a sleep,
An insight that's so deep.
The brain begins to shift,
The facts begin to drift,
Deep subconscious emotions,
Symbol of deadly potions,
In the unconscious mind,
An interpretation that's hard to find.
Impulses of delta waves,
Steady rapid alpha waves,
Such Rapid Eye Movement,
REM is no improvement,
Explaining what a dream creates,
Measuring your heart rates.

Dearly Departed
By: Kass Ghayouri

Loved ones in flight,
Crossed at the light,
They become our guide,
In them we confide,
They visit in a dream,
Our spiritual team.
The dream is so real,
They spiritually heal,
Their spirit so vivid,
Our bodies so livid,
You have this gut feeling,
It's a time of healing.
Their message is clear,
There is no need for fear,
They feel empathy,
A message through telepathy,
They bring you love and peace,
A story of the decease.
They visit to reassure,
They visit just to cure,
They visit to warn,
Appear as early as dawn,
They bring you protection,
With lots of affection.
Your connection with a spirit,
A dream to interpret,
Grandma with gratitude,
Grandpa with attitude,
They visit from beyond,
Memories are so fond.

The Pride of Persia
By: Kass Ghayouri

Horse racing is the game,
Pride of Persia is the name,
Of this powerful horse,
Galloping on the race course,
The owner is so proud,
Leading it through the crowd.
The jockey strikes the whip,
The gates gently flip,
The horse begins to speed,
A specific horse breed,
Gamblers begin to scream,
Winning millions is their dream.
The Durban July Handicap,
Horses run an entire lap,
Fashonisters prance their rounds,
Eccentric fashion on the grounds,
They all appear to be royalty,
Pride of Persia shows loyalty.
The owner gently pats the horse,
A winner he will definitely endorse,
He knows he would win the race,
Pride of Persia in first place,
It is such a spiritual feeling,
To the owner it is a spiritual healing.
Punters make their generous bet,
The horses speed like a moving jet,
Grayville Race course's annual race,
A South African elegant event to embrace,
He hugs his horse with compassion,
Horse racing he loved with such passion!

Kass Ghayouri

Unwanted Dream
By: Kass Ghayouri

I began to scream,
Yet it was only a dream,
I was viciously chased,
I ran with such haste,
I did not have a voice,
I had to make a choice,
Stuck in an intense maze,
I was in a sleepy daze,
The wind began to howl,
The monster began to prowl,
Furiously I began to sweat,
All my bed sheets were wet,
Violently I bumped my head,
As I sat up on my bed,
I heard the dogs bark,
My room was so dark,
Then I saw a ghost,
Sitting at my bed post,
It pulled out my sheet,
Exposing my shaky feet,
Flying over was an orb,
Someone turned my door knob,
The closet door began to rattle,
This was a no win battle,
Shadows walked in my room,
I was in a state of doom,
A pale porcelain doll said, "Hi",
I began to hysterically cry,
Foot steps came up the stairs,
Like soldiers stood my hairs,
My voice went on strike,
A nightmare I did not like,
A matter of fight or flight,
I sat so still with fright,
A man at my window,

A friend or maybe a foe,
He had a sly grin,
Looking for his next of kin,
A static voice said, "Out.",
I began to cry and pout,
I felt a sudden cold breeze,
My whole body began to freeze,
A strange black mass apparition,
They had a strange mission,
My door bell then rang,
I saw a monster with a fang,
He began to silently moan,
I began to hysterically groan,
A cat began to scratch,
Someone opened the front door latch,
It was a headless stranger,
I was in intense danger,
Tormented with this dream,
I gave out a blood wrenching scream,
Psychological and physical terror,
Despair, anxiety and then horror,
I leapt out of my bed,
Surrounded by the dead,
Ran down the spiral staircase,
Perspiration running down my face,
I turned on the kitchen light,
That put an end to the fright,
All spiritual activities were gone,
It was the break of dawn,
Paranormal activities were gone,
Left with a feeling of forlorn.

Metaphysics
By: Kass Ghayouri

A branch of philosophy,
Like a branch of a tree,
It is an encyclopedia,
Explaining strange notions,
Space, time, cause and effect,
It has an answer for all.

It delivers knowledge,
Like a mailman with mail,
It is the history of science,
Rejected by natural science,
The fundamental nature of being,
Can metaphysics explain all?

Questions existence and reality,
Questions the mind and matter,
Opinions of religion and spirituality,
What is space and time?
Can it explain existence and objects?
What is metaphysics?

Metaphysic's brother is ontology,
Knows the categories of being,
Metaphysic's sister is cosmology,
Knows the dynamics of the universe,
Natural philosophy is the mother,
Providing the family with knowledge.

Spring Clean your Relationships
By: Kass Ghayouri

Spring has arrived!
Renewal and rebirth,
You spring clean your home,
Got rid of that junk,
Kept what is needed,
Got rid of the useless.

Spring has arrived!
Spring clean relationships,
Get rid of those friends,
Those that use you,
Even those that abuse you,
The ones that back stab.

Friends that are jealous,
Wearing a cloak with a dagger,
Friends that are envious,
Wearing that friendly mask,
Ones that gossip behind your back,
They belong behind your back.

Spring has arrived!
It is time to move forward,
Get rid of the superficial friends,
Clear that negative path,
Make room for new friends,
It is a spiritual cleansing.

Kass Ghayouri

Positive Thinking
By: Kass Ghayouri

Negative thoughts bring you pain,
Then you have nothing to gain,
Your energy will always drain,
Like a weight sitting on your brain,
Do not walk down that negative lane,
It will really drive you insane!

Falling prey to a negative thought,
In a negative web you are caught,
A feeling of being distraught,
It's negative energy you brought,
Negative messages you have to sought,
As a child that's what I've been taught.

Now focus on positive thinking,
Meditation and yoga without blinking,
Try to smile without frowning,
It is mental and spiritual healing,
During stress there are ways of coping,
Avoid depression, distress and moping.

You can positively control how you feel,
Feeling empowered is a positive deal,
Reflect on positive thoughts and you will heal,
Find good positive friendships to seal,
Being paranoid is like eating a junk meal,
Like a fishing rod those positive friends you reel.

Kass Ghaypuris

Law of Attraction
By: Kass Ghayouri

You are a magnet,
The power to attract,
You belong in a universe,
You are in full control,
The power is in your hands,
You have the power to ask,
Universe does not decline,
It generously gives,
You gratefully take,
Positive thinking draws!
It brings you good health,
It brings you wealth,
Your mind is a basket,
You fill it with thoughts,
My basket is filled,
With prosperity and health,
With happiness and wealth,
With love and luck,
Security, success, intelligence,
Peace of mind and power!
It's time to fill your basket,
With a magnet of thoughts,
Deliver the filled basket,
To the powerful universe,
It will wholeheartedly give,
Like an ocean full of water,
The universe has abundance,
It is ready to give,
Whatever your heart desires,
Transmission through thoughts,
Rings a bell in the universe,
Like a store catalogue,
You order and it sends!

Envy
By: Kass Ghayouri

An envious potion,
Full of evil emotion,
What a person lacks,
They gossip behind backs,
Like snakes they slither,
Oh dear they come hither!
You cannot really deny,
It is called the evil eye,
Inflicting misfortune on you,
What can you really do?
Envy is so negative,
Jinx on all that's positive,
Envious about your wealth,
Brings you poor health,
Envious about your success,
Wanting you to have less,
Envious about your marriage,
Travelling in an envious carriage,
Then they silently curse,
Envy your designer purse,
Their envy burns like fire,
The symptom of desire,
You rise with such hope,
With envy they cannot cope,
It's a disastrous emotion,
They envy your promotion,
Their mind loses balance,
Envy, a negative valance,
Envy controls their mind,
Sincere friends are hard to find,
Your past karmic action,
Brings financial satisfaction,
Beware of the evil eye!
Break away from the evil tie!

Kaos Ghayouri

Praying Mantis
By: Kass Ghayouri

As green as the grass,
It holds up its fore- limbs,
In a prayer like position,
It perched on my window ledge,
A spiritual messenger of God,
With its spiritual power.

Mantis in Greek for prophet,
It brings mystical powers,
I observe its enormous eyes,
An allusion of God's presence,
Looking though those eyes,
It's here to guide my way.

It points out God's direction,
Such a spiritual creature,
It acts as a compass,
It is a symbolic preacher,
It points the way to heaven,
A foundation of spirit.

I am fascinated by its posture,
It prays to a spiritual light,
A green, gazing, God like symbol,
Symbolizing strength and power,
A pondering, praying pest,
An enlightening spiritual guest.

Kass Ghayouri

The Owl
By: Kass Ghayouri

The spirit of an Owl,
It is present to guide,
Bringing me wisdom,
And intuitive knowledge,
Takes me beyond deceit,
Transition to a new life.

How can I ignore such power?
It warns me of deception,
Illusion, the cunning and crude,
I evaluate true reality,
Of those ulterior motives,
Dishonesty of those around me.

The Owl is my spirit guide,
The Owl is my magician,
It is my sincere bodyguard,
It sharpens my intuitive mind,
Brings out my hidden potential,
It nurtures my creative energy.

The Owl showed up in my life,
To bring about positive change,
It showed up in my dream,
Symbolic of a deceased energy,
To protect and guide me,
I am now filled with wisdom.

My Spiritual Self
By: Kass Ghayouri

In touch with my spiritual self,
It is like a juice and food blender,
I put in my psychological thoughts,
Together with my mystical nature,
My personal development and moral self,
My spiritual experience and knowledge,
A blend of religion and faith,
My purity, wisdom, and existence,
All blended into a spiritual smoothie.

I transformed it into a magic potion,
My personal blend of humanistic psychology,
I topped it with delicate spices,
To enhance the taste and create the mood,
Spices of devotion and mental health,
Universal power, planetary action, motive,
Love, affection, feeling and appreciation,
I now have my super spiritual tonic,
The psychology of this spiritual drink.

The drink flows down my digestive track,
The taste of mysticism and truth,
I digest the power of my spirituality,
I taste the structure of self-awareness,
I have ingested the discovery of higher power,
My blended juice provides me with energy,
A consciousness of self and liberation,
My true nature of what is reality.
I am now content with my spiritual self!

Jealousy
By: Kass Ghayouri

We live in a world of jealousy,
The nature of the human mind,
As you progress up in life,
A gravitation force pulls you down,
It is not the force of nature,
But the force of that jealous mind.

It's like walking the surface of earth,
You successfully go up in life,
Yet that jealous one pulls you down,
Do not pay attention to their force,
Continue to climb up in life,
Reach out and be that famous star.

Jealous people in a black hole,
A space in time preventing their escape,
They look at you with the evil eye,
Their obnoxious sense of sight,
Their emotions and negative thoughts,
Insecurity, resentment and anger.

What triggers such jealous minds?
That leads to threats and violence,
That insecure personality trait,
With enormous, emotional envy,
Your steady secure success,
Provide them with a punching bag!

Luck
By: Kass Ghayouri

Whatever I touch turns to gold,
My mystical touch is so bold,
I always get what I desire,
My spiritual luck is on fire,
I have found my clover leaf,
My luck is now in disbelief.

Luck brought me fortune and fame,
Prosperity, profit and a good name,
Bestowed with help from the divine,
Fortunate luck is now all mine,
Good karma set in my path,
Removing all negative and evil wrath.

In my life I generously gave,
Those in trouble I always save,
My belief is always optimistic,
None of my thoughts are pessimistic,
Good karma comes with a good deed,
Always helping those in great need.

I executed all positive action,
Good luck brings so much satisfaction,
A four-leaf clover that's so rare,
Faith, hope, love, luck is what I bare,
Spiritual showering of pixie dust,
Positive thinking is also a must.

Spiritual Love
By: Kass Ghayouri

Present at my faithful birth,
You placed me on this earth,
Yet you did not want to stay,
I remember that horrific day,
You approached to say goodbye,
Apologizing it was time to die,
You would not abide by my request,
Wanting no part of your bequest,
Thought I'd see biological aging,
Our conversation was so engaging,
You took me by utter surprise,
Your soulful spirit had to rise,
Heavenly light of the bright tunnel,
Angels at the end of the funnel,
Experience of spiritual progression,
Left me with solemn confession,
I begged you to reenter your body,
You would not confide in anybody,
You hastened through a spiritual portal,
A demise that is spiritually mortal,
Traumatized and in such distress,
Grieving is a spiritual process,
Leaving me with histrionic sobs,
Dear father I see your spirit in orbs,
In a pearl like light you appear,
Your spiritual message is so clear,
Reassurance and peace of mind,
Your gracious spirit I often find,
Over the spiritual realm and light,
You visit in dreams at night,
It's your unconditional love,
I spiritually receive from above!
Your orbs in a photograph,
I will recite your autograph.

Kass Ghayouri

Family Bond
By: Kass Ghayouri

A nuclear family,
Form a special bond,
With spiritual love,
Unbreakable ties,
And mutual respect,
Interactive process,
Special attachment,
Providing affection,
Unconditional trust,
Working in harmony,
A higher form of love,
Working for happiness,
Gift of good fortune,
A family bondage,
As strong as gold,
Sparkles like a diamond,
A family union,
A chemical equation,
A passionate family tie,
God bless this family,
Their emotional bond,
Protect them against envy,
Strengthen their bond,
Maternal bond of stability,
Paternal bond of affection,
Dynamics of a family,
A family to treasure,
With enduring love,
Sharing special time,
Sharing communication,
The foundation of bonding,
Its compatible values,
Seals the spiritual bond!

I am Intellectually Tall
By: Kass Ghayouri

I am physically short,
Yet I'm intellectually tall,
You stand like a tower,
Yet I am able to empower,
Watch my creative energy flow,
Observe my intellectual curiosity grow,
I am the epitome of success,
A personification of progress,
As I climb the intellectual rung,
Moral anguish of an envious stung,
Yes I play the confidence game,
Being short is not to blame.

I am physically short,
Yet I'm intellectually tall,
Let's not measure physical height,
And get into a superficial fight,
Let's measure intelligence quotient,
Sadly your knowledge is deficient,
There's no room to be insecure,
Insult mongers are just not pure,
I cannot stop to release an arrow,
A prejudice mind that's so narrow,
The prosperous ladder I ascend,
With no obligation to ever descend.

Children's
Poetry

Kindergarten Rap
By: Kass Ghayouri

It's a kindergarten rap,
Wear your baseball cap,
Let's move to the beat,
Shake your little feet,
You can sing along,
To our happy rap song,
You can sing aloud,
Your mom will be proud,
Open up your lips,
Also move those hips,
Move to the far right,
Let's sing until midnight,
Our voices have to be strong,
Our song has to be long,
The words have to rhyme,
The bells chime!

A Poem
By: Kass Ghayouri

Once upon a time,
A poem with a rhyme,
All about a little child,
That's happy and wild,
He always loved to run,
He loved to have fun,
He also loved to swing,
Then he would sing,
He played with a kite,
His paper kite was light,
He kicked his soccer ball,
On the grass he would fall,
He loved all his toys,
He played with other boys,
All he did was play,
Each and every day!

Haiku Poem
By: Kass Ghayouri

Lots of books to read,
Turning pages of each book,
A daily routine.

Interesting words,
Pictures that pop right at you,
Relaxing reading.

Black ink on paper,
The story continues on,
A suspense drama.

Let us read indeed,
A book with a thousand words,
Enjoy the story.

Acrostic Poem
By: Kass Ghayouri

Books filled with knowledge,
Academic information for success,
Carrying heavy loads,
Kilograms of school equipment.
Packing for school each morning,
Also affects the posture,
Cloth bag with such strength,
Keeps books organized.

Homework assignments,
Outside the classroom,
Mainly to increase knowledge,
Education spells out success,
Writing essays and journals,
Other skills to study,
Reading to improve vocabulary,
Know how to higher our grades.

Studying each day,
Claims to educate children,
Homework improves skills,
Organizing academic work,
On-line research work,
Learning different subjects.

Limerick Poem
By: Kass Ghayouri

She was so simple,
Her cheek had a dimple,
Her eyes were squint,
It was covered in lint,
Her nose had a big pimple.

She was a drama queen,
She caused a dramatic scene,
Each time she would cry,
Mucus from her nose would fly,
It landed on the Dean.

There was a tiny mouse,
He lived in a tiny house,
He always scratched his head,
Thinking the louse was dead,
His friend was a tiny louse.

He went to the bank
With his machine tank,
He held up the teller,
He was a mortgage seller,
He tried to pull a prank.

Kass Ghaypuri

Definition Poetry
By: Kass Ghayouri

What is saving?
    It is putting away money,
    In a piggy bank or bank,
    It is saving for tomorrow,
    An abundance of wealth,
    It is making yourself rich,
    A responsibility to save,
    Saving money over the years,
    Can bring you happiness and joy,
    You can buy that luxury car,
    And that beautiful mansion too,
    You can travel around the world,
    Meeting different people and cultures,
    You will have enough money to spend,
    Put away those pennies each day,
    You will save for your future,
    And be rich too!
That is saving!

A Story Plot
By: Kass Ghayouri

A story plot is like a slide,
The story begins with events,
We meet all the characters,
We know their personal traits,
We are introduced to the setting.
Then there is the rising action,
It is the ladder of the slide,
As the story moves higher up,
It becomes more complicated,
As we ascend the ladder it is scary.
We arrive at the climax,
It is the top of the slide,
It is also the main problem,
And the highest point of interest,
This part of the slide is full of suspense.
The story takes us to the falling action,
This is when the problem gets solved,
Just like sliding it moves so fast,
The conflict is then settled,
Characters reach a resolution.
The story draws to a fascinating end,
The end may be happy or sad,
It is like falling onto the sand,
Characters know the answer to the problem,
The ride on the slide comes to an end.

Winter Tongue Twister
By: Kass Ghayouri

Winter's wild weather,
Why was winter wild?
Which way winter wobbles?
When winter whisked,
With wild, weird, winds,
Where women worried?
Who walked with winter?
Who was winter with?
What was winter welcoming?
Women wore weathered woolies,
Warm weather went West,
When winter wondered,
Western winds whistled,
While winter winds whizzed,
Wavy, wind, wacky, whirlwinds,
We wonder why winter wanders,
Wholesome white winter weather,
Wildlife went wondering,
We would worry whether,
When winter whirls west,
Worldwide wet weird weather,
We whine with weird winter!

Father
By: Kass Ghayouri

Dad, daddy, papa, pa, pop,
With my dad I jump and hop,
Together we would race,
He runs at a fast pace,
Dad is my present and past,
My love for him will always last,
Dad is always by my side,
In dad I can always confide,
My love for him is so deep,
He tucks me in when I sleep,
He takes me to the park,
He protects me in the dark,
Dad always makes my day,
He listens to what I say,
He knows how to discipline me,
When I'm naughty as you can see,
He knows when I make a mistake,
Dad is so good and never fake,
He does not have an easy task,
Putting on the father mask,
A father's work is never done,
Being a dad is so much fun,
My dad knows what I need,
He is the best father indeed,
A soccer game and movie night,
What he says is always right,
Sometimes he has no time for me,
He works so hard, I can see,
He taught me how to ride my bike,
That's what I will always like,
I know he will always care,
Dad is always kind and fair!

Kass Ghayoun

Mother
By: Kass Ghayouri

Mom makes a sacrifice,
She is loving, caring, and nice,
I am her special child,
Although I am sometimes wild,
A mother's love is a good gift,
My spirit she will always lift,
She is there when there is wrong,
Mom is so intelligent and strong,
She buys me what I need,
I love my mom so much, indeed,
I can go to her for advice,
She bought me my electronic device,
When I go into my hard shell,
Mom always checks that I am well,
In times of trouble she is calm,
She protects me from any harm,
My mom will love me forever,
Loving me now and whenever,
She spends valuable time with me,
Makes me as happy as can be,
With valuable time we bond,
Mom shows me that she's fond,
Teaches me to be independent,
To try not to be dependent,
Encourages me to be successful,
Making sure that I am respectful,
Unconditional love and acceptance,
Gives me freedom and confidence,
Teaches me to be honest and kind,
A mom like mine is hard to find,
Mom is my very first teacher,
My lecturer, instructor and preacher.

Responsibility
By: Kass Ghayouri

I have the ability,
To show lots of responsibility,
To get good grades at school,
Education is an important tool,
I will make a good time table,
Because I am independent and able.
I will always clean my room,
To vacuum, wash and groom,
See that my homework is completed,
And all my bad habits are deleted,
I will study on my own,
To show I am mature and grown.
All my allowance I will save,
I will be strong and also brave,
Always be early and never late,
Remember deadlines and a date,
Always read each and every night,
At bedtime turn off the light.
After saving I can spend,
Spending and saving have to blend,
I will see that I am never broke,
My life will not be a joke,
I will take charge of what I need,
I will be so responsible, indeed.

Stranger Danger
By: Kass Ghayouri

Be careful of a stranger,
It can be a danger,
You have to keep walking,
A stranger may be stalking,
Do not walk away alone,
You can always use a phone.
A stranger is like a hawk,
Always wanting to stalk,
A stranger you do not know,
He can be an enemy and a foe,
On children they can prey,
From your mom do not stray.
A stranger can be good and bad,
Strangers can be happy and sad,
Uncomfortable is what you feel,
With strangers you learn to deal,
You can always walk away,
Do not listen to what he has to say.
Tell an adult that you trust,
Keeping yourself safe is a must,
When a stranger touches you – scream,
Like the monster in your dream.
Ignore and run really fast,
The staying safe rule at last.
They offer you food or candy,
Remembering rules are handy,
They make you take a bet,
To first find their loving pet,
You really cannot go along,
Being with a stranger is so wrong!

You Are So Special
By: Kass Ghayouri

You're a special little girl,
With your wiggles and twirl,
As beautiful as a rose,
Love to watch you pose,
Your eyes sparkle like stars,
So different like planet Mars,
Your nose is really pretty,
You are so funny and witty,
I love the way you talk,
You have a fairy like walk,
Love the color of your skin,
And your fantastic grin,
I love the way you sing,
It is like a cell phone ring,
And the special way you dance,
You give that cute, sly glance,
You are intelligent or smart,
And your kind and loving heart,
I see your beautiful face,
You belong to a magical race,
I hear your amazing voice,
You are a friend of my choice,
I smell your perfume scent,
When we play in the tent,
I touch your smooth hand,
When we sing in the school band,
You will always be the best,
And you are loved by the rest!

Diamante Poems
The Beach
By: Kass Ghayouri

Beach
Warm, beautiful
Splashing, Playing, Swimming
This feeling is freedom
Sunbathing, fishing, eating
Sparkling, Exotic
Pool

Waves
Fluffy, Foamy
Rolling, Surfing, Splashing
Excitedly splashing in waves
Riding, winding, jumping
Humid, Salty
Water

Sand
Sparkling, Wet
Building, playing, making
The amazing sand castles
Splashing, lifting, digging
Fantastic, Exotic
Rocks

Cinquains Poem
By: Kass Ghayouri

Fairy Tale
Princess
So beautiful
Dancing like a fairy
She is feeling so excited
Maiden

Handsome
So enchanting
Dancing and gliding too
So much in love with the princess
Wedding

Dancing
At the Royal Ball
All night ballroom dancing
Staring into each other's eyes
Moving

Story
Prince and Princess
A story about love
Falling in love is so easy
A tale

Good Manners
By: Kass Ghayouri

Good manners are important,
A good personality trait,
You should always say please,
Then followed by thank you,
Do not speak with your mouthful,
Do not interrupt when others speak,
It's bad to listen to adult's conversation,
Do not get involved in adult matters.

Be polite and kind to others,
Help them when they are in need,
Be generous and share with others,
Your toys, books, food and more,
Have respect for adults and friends,
Treat them with care, kindness and love,
Do not gossip behind their backs,
Share your opinion and feelings too.

With good manners you are accepted,
With good manners you are respected,
With good manners you are special,
With good manners you are appreciated,
With good manners you get attention,
With good manners you get affection,
With good manners you are loved,
With good manners you're the best!

You are a Hero!
By: Kass Ghayouri

A handsome little boy,
That brings so much joy,
You are so energetic,
Your personality so electric,
I see a Super Hero in you,
And you are special too,
A little boy that's strong,
Always right and never wrong,
A boy that is so brave,
And with a friendly wave,
As courageous as Batman,
As amazing as Superman,
As strong as Incredible Hulk,
Have games in such a bulk,
Like Green Lantern you arrive,
Like a dragon you dive,
You are an incredible child,
Like a lion that is so wild,
Like a monkey on a tree,
You are as happy as can be,
Like a big strong polar bear,
You always love and care,
Most of all you are super smart,
A little boy with a big heart,
At school you do your best,
Getting good grades on a test,
You always love to read,
You are so special indeed,
You are daddy's little champ,
Sending your cars down a ramp,
You are mom's little sport,
Parking your cars in a carport,
Dear little handsome boy,
You deserve a special toy.

Reach for the Stars!
By: Kass Ghayouri

Don't let anyone put you down,
Or look at you and frown,
If they say you are bad,
Now they are really sad,
If they say you're not smart,
They have a terrible heart,
If they say you're useless,
Then they have to be senseless,
Show them that you will rise,
Now take my positive advice,
In life you go higher and higher,
You are someone that we admire,
Climb up that success ladder,
Slither up like a puff adder,
For the stars you have to reach,
Listen to what I have to teach,
Climb the success ladder really fast,
Like a space rocket you blast,
Do not stop to throw stones,
At jealous people with nasty tones,
Stopping will make you go slow,
Envious people want to keep you low,
You have all the determination,
Do not let it be a termination,
Determination means a good goal,
You want to reach the North Pole,
Termination means to stop,
That will make you drop,
Reach out for the blue sky,
You have to really try,
Reach out and touch the stars,
Like riding in fast cars!

Life can be a Struggle!
By: Kass Ghayouri

Yes, I understand,
Life can be planned,
Life can be a struggle,
You are able to juggle,
All your subjects at school,
Education an important tool,
As stubborn as a mule,
Life has a special rule,
Having to work hard,
A rule you cannot discard,
Put in your very best,
Do better than the rest,
It's like climbing a tree,
It's like getting a degree,
You cannot give up,
You have lots in your cup,
Now motivate yourself,
A teacher can really help,
To help you to success,
Do not give into stress,
As you climb to the top,
Make sure you do not drop,
Like climbing that tree,
You want to be free,
Hang on to those branches,
Life is about taking chances,
Do not say it's impossible,
You have to be responsible,
You have to be independent,
That's what life intended!

Always Help Others!
By: Kass Ghayouri

The story of Robin Hood,
A character that is good,
He gets money from the rich,
He crosses the forest bridge,
He gave money to the poor,
Knocking at their house door.

You can also help another,
Mom, dad, friend, sister or brother,
Always help those in need,
It is really good karma indeed,
Listen to what they have to say,
A skill that will make their day.

Volunteer at the food bank,
Not everyone has a good rank,
Homeless people you can feed,
Do not go through life with greed,
Fundraisers will help them too,
Even something small will do.

Volunteer at an old aged center,
Into their lives you will enter,
There are people that are alone,
All you need is to pick up a phone,
Call them just to say that you care,
Finding a loyal friend is rare.

Homeless children at a shelter,
They need a good and loyal protector,
These children need books and toys,
Give donations to these girls and boys,
Help others with an open mind,
One like you is hard to find.

Nursery Rhymes
By: Kass Ghayouri

One, two, three, four, five,
Bring back the nursery rhyme,
It is all about time,
Make my rhyme come alive!

Three, four, five, six, seven,
Mom and dad sing with me,
I am happy as you can see,
This is like being in heaven.

Eight, nine, ten, and eleven,
It's time to go out to play,
This is going to be a good day,
We can go back to seven.

Twelve, thirteen, fourteen, fifteen,
Playing on the playground,
Going on the merry-go-round,
Hey friends where have you been.

Sixteen, seventeen, eighteen, nineteen,
We have to learn how to read,
To be smart that's what we need,
Children have to be heard and seen.

Lyrics
By: Kass Ghayouri

Let's get together to write a song,
It does not have to be so long,
All we need is a unique style,
It may even take a while,
Let's open up our mind's eye,
Let the words sincerely fly.

It will be a creative venture,
It will be a successful adventure,
Let's write with a specific intention,
Our inner emotions we can mention,
Songwriting takes so much time,
Trying to make each line rhyme,

I would love to express my feelings,
Words of a song can be so healing,
Let's avoid what is depressing,
Those feelings can be suppressing,
Laying on my comfortable bed,
All these words come to my head.

Now we have all our amazing lines,
With an interesting sound that combines,
We need a melody and a beat,
Turn up the volume and feel the heat,
A chorus that repeats without change,
I found a chorus with a vocal range,

Now let us challenge our skills,
We need to take those magical pills,
Or even try to sprinkle pixie dust,
An unforgettable song is always a must,
Like salad with tasty seasoning,
My song has such intelligent reasoning.

English Course
By: Kass Ghayouri

English is a strange subject,
Unique thoughts to project,
Then the teacher gives a grade,
The lotto 649 that is played,
One teacher gives a ninety,
The other brings it down to seventy.

It's like playing a lottery,
As difficult as making pottery,
A student's potential does not change,
A grade falls down that is strange,
The teacher's marking is not stable,
Does the student get a label?

An assignment given to different teachers,
Following all the essay features,
One English teacher gives a ninety-five,
Then another teacher gives a seventy-five,
Is that just a teacher's bias?
Marked by hypocrisy or being pious.

This leaves the student confused,
Is the marking rubric being misused?
Student tries to find an explanation,
With the teacher there is no negotiation,
Is the teacher being fair with grades?
Parents seek for excellent tutorial aids.

They lose faith in certain schools,
Not using fair educational tools,
The drop in marks is so absurd,
Unbelievable at what has occurred,
It is the teacher's personality trait,
This becomes an educational debate.

A Teacher's Note
By: Kass Ghayouri

This is a teacher's note,
Hop onto my educational boat,
Together we will calmly sail,
Believe me! You will never fail,
I will sacrifice my time,
Even sacrificing that dime,
Doing my educational part,
Coming from the bottom of my heart,
I always teach with passion,
Giving students my compassion,
Having a bold, intelligent voice,
Helping you make a positive choice,
My focus is on what you learn,
Higher grades you will surely earn,
There is no need to shiver,
The curriculum I will deliver,
At a slow and interesting pace,
Great knowledge you will embrace,
I will not let your marks drop,
Promise you will never flop,
Providing you with a major skill,
That curious mind I will fill,
Being a responsible member of society,
Educational methods with a variety,
Let me take your strong hand,
Your intelligence will expand,
We will form an educational team,
Watch how I higher your self esteem,
A teacher that will make a difference,
Avoiding all negative interference,
There is only one of me to go around,
That sincere teacher you have found!

It is not Wrong to Write!
By: Kass Ghayouri

I sat on the right,
All ready to write,
I sat there stationary,
With all my stationery,
I wondered whether...
Should I write about the weather?
I began to clearly see,
Images of a blue sea,
I gently scratched my hair,
Think as fast as a hare,
I began to softly hear,
The waves not far from here,
The old clock struck two,
I could smell the ocean too,
The time just passed,
I thought about my past,
Basking in the hot sun,
With a friend and her son,
Admiring the sky so blue,
Observing the bubbles he blew,
Buzzing around was a bee,
We were as happy as can be,
Those were amazing days,
Just sitting in a daze,
Watching the ships sail,
Vendors had items for sale,
Each had their own site,
The beach was a pleasant sight,
I did not know what to buy,
As desperate vendors walked by,
The time was now close to eight,
My dinner I had ate,
Surfers on a surf board,
Excited and never bored,
Tourist descended the stairs,

There were lots of stares,
I just greeted with a "Hi",
Watching the waves so high,
Observing the waves break,
Listen to the car brake,
People on a boat cruise,
With entertaining crews,
The water came up to my waist,
These memories I cannot waste,
A carriage ride to hire,
Waves went higher and higher,
What a beautiful scene,
The best I'd ever seen,
A tug with a ship in tow,
Buried in the sand my toe,
In the sand I made a hole,
The yellow sand as a whole,
A holiday I had won,
A holiday that was number one,
I played with a beach pail,
A tan for those who are pale,
I watched the high tide,
Different shells I tied,
This place was so right,
To sit down and write,
A place you cannot be idle,
The surfer is my idol,
My thoughts were so new,
Now I really knew,
You cannot say, "No",
To such beauty you know,
The Indian Ocean and I,
No blinking of the eye.

Seperation and Divorce!
By: Kass Ghayouri

Your feelings will change,
That is really not strange,
Sometimes you are sad,
Other times angry or mad,
There is no easy solution,
However there is a resolution,
You are not to blame,
You cannot feel any shame,
Talk about how you feel,
It is time that will heal,
Friends and family you can trust,
They will help you to adjust,
You have nothing to fear,
As bad as it may appear,
Handling separation and divorce,
You cannot feel remorse,
Adults have made a decision,
You have all the supervision,
You will not be alone,
A family member on the phone,
Always there to help you cope,
To give you guidance and hope,
Friends, cousins, uncles and aunts,
Available to listen to your rants,
Always maintain that connection,
Providing you with protection,
To fill your life with love and joy,
Family life you will enjoy,
You will be in a safe place,
Compassion and love to embrace,
You have unconditional love,
Spiritual guidance from above.

Your Child is NOT your Friend
By: Kass Ghayouri

"I am my child's best friend",
Let's bring that phrase to an end,
You cannot play a friend's role,
As a parent you have a goal,
Parenting is raising a child,
Raising a best friend is wild,
You need to give parental care,
Calling a child a friend is not fair,
A friend you cannot rear,
That message is so clear,
Calling your child a friend is wrong,
That message is cognitively strong,
A child you need to control,
You need to play the parental role,
You have to set an explicit rule,
Punishment is an effective tool,
Dealing with a child's deviance,
Listening to a parent's grievance,
Show a child who's in charge,
Bad behaviors you cannot discharge,
In a friend you often confide,
Adult issues from a child you hide,
Problems with a friend you share,
These problems are not a child's affair,
Parents teach self-regulation,
With parents there's little negotiation,
Calling a child a friend is a mistake,
Rules from you they will not take,
A friend is someone their own age,
A child has their own development stage,
Your friend should be mature,
Not a child that's so immature.

A Feisty Toy!
By: Kass Ghayouri

As cute as a toy,
A pet for a girl or a boy,
Just loving adventure,
What a joint venture!
An amazing companion,
A pet in a million,
Energetic, loyal and brave,
Always there to save,
When you are in trouble,
It's there in a double,
So energetic and wild,
Often like a little child,
Affectionate to its master,
Ideal for a youngster,
Craving for attention,
Jealous behavior to mention,
It is so easy to train,
Discipline and restrain,
A leader of the pack,
Always having your back,
That cute little size,
What a precious prize!
Always wants to play,
Leader leads the way,
A trendy shaggy look,
Hiding in every nook,
A really unique breed,
Adorable and amazing indeed,
Glamorous and feisty,
Loving with honesty,
Vivacious in spirit,
Deserving a high merit,
It's the Yorkshire Terrier,
A recessive gene carrier.

Classical Dancing
By: Kass Ghayouri

Soulful and liberating,
Evoking all the senses,
A royal form of art,
Exotic facial expressions,
Unique hand gestures,
Narrating a story line.

Calling on emotions,
Indian classical dance,
Different forms and styles,
Like thunder the foot stomps,
Like lightening lights flash,
A top spinning with force.

It's a God and a Goddess,
Entertaining the deities,
Art of Bharata Natyam,
Eyeballs rolling like marbles,
Knees bent at a right angle,
The talent of a culture.

In Hindu mythology,
Symbolic of each deity,
Creation and destruction,
Cosmic and functional,
Dance is the form of worship,
Reveals mythological tales.

The greeting of a God,
The slaying of a villain,
Welcoming such royalty,
Highlighting a festival,
The Indian art of dancing,
With singing and drumming.

East meets the west,
The tone is set,
The mood is revised,
The dramatic monologue begins,
Violin, flute, and drums,
With music and a beat.

The snake silently slithers,
A prelude to a drama,
The drum violently beats,
A hero then emerges,
And saves the maiden.

With glamorous costumes,
With colorful attire,
With vibrant face paint,
Hair like a spring garden,
Tattoo on hands and feet,
The essence of classical dance.

The Helicopter Parent
By: Kass Ghayouri

Like a flying helicopter,
The parent hovers over the child,
Removing all independence,
Creating only dependence,
They become hyper-present,
With ridiculous control.

A teacher's worst nightmare,
The parent does the homework,
The homework earns a lower grade,
The parent charges like a bull,
Impeach, impede, imperative, impolite,
Heckles with questions and taunts.

Like a marshal the coach disciplines,
Preparing players to win the game,
Failure and challenge brings success,
The parent hovers over the coach,
Hurling threats and physical abuse,
A form of Munchausen Syndrome.

Over parenting, overprotecting, over controlling,
Shadowing the child's movements,
Excessive attention and monitoring,
Parenting governed by immense fear,
The child cannot master any skill,
The helicopter parent hovers over.

Made in the USA
Charleston, SC
01 October 2016